Eclipsing Entries

Madison Lucchesi

BookLeaf Publishing

Fabric & String

I am of fabric of string.
I am of rips, tears, and scars.

The patches of my life:
my color coded calendar,
excessive studying,
prompt homework submissions,
and inability to halt productivity,
Are sewn tight enough to mask the effects of
my grandmother's death,
surviving a trauma,
high-functioning anxiety,
and the rifts between my family and I,
from my entire circle.

Most days break me, but I stitch myself up
and sew on a bright smile.

Me in Pieces

I speak four languages, none of which are
conventional

I speak one of food through
Cherishing the fragility of snickerdoodle cookie
dough
Craving the greasy comfort of a double
cheeseburger
and side of fries
Dreaming to be as simple and robust as
seven course Italian meals
Admiring the cilantro and lime duet found in
Hispanic dishes
as perfect as friendships should be
Desiring the warmth and familiarity of sushi
Remembering the sting of ice cream
in my lactose intolerant stomach
Asking to be compassionate and comforting
like every dish that has passed through my hands

I speak one of movies and tv shows through
Becoming fluent in blockbuster one liners
Studying every classic by anyone from
Quentin Tarantino to Steven Spielberg

Predicting the end of every Grey's Anatomy episode
Praying to be as funny as Kate McKinnon
Memorizing every line in On the Basis of Sex
Knowing actors for all of their roles, stupendous or putrid
Sobbing when a character is grieving because I am too
Referencing Gilmore Girls and Friends lines
in my day to day conversations

I speak one of love through
Putting my exhausted mother to bed every night
Starting random conversations with friends
just so they remember I'm there
Tending to my grandmother and her declining memory
Cancelling plans when my pets are sick
Holding my boyfriend as he grieved his father, his aunt,
and truly the only life he's ever known
Helping my brother write his college essays
Making enough food to distract those in my close circle
from the pain of this past year
Teaching little children to enjoy dance the way I do
Loving others the way I've always wanted to be

I speak one of literature through
Debating To Kill a Mockingbird with every
teacher I can
Describing the books I read as “classics”
(when I was in the fifth grade)
Yearning for enough time to finish a book in one
sitting
just one more time
Trying to broaden my vocabulary in every
conversation
Spreading my proudest pieces on an Instagram
page
Creating for a teen magazine

This

These are the pieces of me, unique and divergent

Ode to My Hair

Multicolored; a blend of my relatives
Red, on my best day, connecting me
To the green fields of my ancestors
Brown, on most days, to mimic the
Mediterranean mountains my
Grandmother grew up on
Blonde, on the warmest days,
To reflect the sunlight and a pot of gold

A thick blanket for my neck in the winter
A pest in the summer heat
A simple trim makes me feel brand new

A reflection of who I am:
Complicated, beautiful and unique

The Best

Every day as I walked past
my Nana's bedroom to go
to school, she reminded me
to, "Be the Best!," in a cheery voice,
even on the grey-est days.

And every day when I came
home from school, she'd ask,
"Were you the best today?"

The answer was always yes.

It's been two years since
I've heard those words.
I miss them.
I long for them.

After my Nana passed,
my Nonna began to tell
me, "You are the best!,"
in her Italian accent.

My Nonna has kept
that tradition, that legacy
alive without even knowing it.

Those words are
etched in my soul
and one day, they'll
be etched in my skin
Because I am always
My Best.

Redamancy

Redamancy

the act of loving in return

My Nonna is the kindest woman I know
and the woman I aspire to be most.
She never thinks I am warm enough
or have had enough to eat.
She has offered me both the food off her plate
and the sweater off her back.
Even in the 90 degree heat,
she chases me with socks and sweaters.

One Christmas, she gave me a sweater
that she knit for my aunt many moons ago.
Every time I see her, she offers to hand wash the
sweater.
She is 85 years old and spends most of her days
in her
heated, reclining chair.

I cannot offer her my tiny sweaters, but
I can warm her with heated blankets, with a cup
of tea,

and most of all,
with my love.

Mirror, Mirror

What do you see?
Is it more than just a reflection?
Can you see what I will be;
What is beyond my skin?
Do you know ALL the broken
pieces of me?
Can you sense my emotions;
Hear my amplified thoughts?
Do YOU know me best?
What will this world make of me?
Am I the one looking back at me?

Day and Night

As the vibrant tangerine sun
Rises over the glistening
Cerulean ocean waves in
The morning,
The reflection staring back
At me has never
Been more vulnerable.
Untouched by the outside elements,
Yet puffy, creased and pink from the
Anxious somersaulting gymnastics
Routine I rehearse in my bed every night.
I stand there, simply beautiful,
Nothing more.
The day has yet to reshape me into
Something gorgeous.

After the lavender sun has fallen and the
Speckled sky has awaken, my tired body
Has never been so stunning.
Each day is the rehearsal of my dance routine:
leaping toward feelings, turning to learning, and
tapping for debating.
The routine, day in and day out, will wear on
you,
But it will create an even better person.

My nightly reflection is what I am
Most proud of.

The Experiment

Scientists control us all
Looking down from huge mechanisms
Adjusting people
Planning who they'll meet
Experimenting with their limits
Testing what they can take
Hurting them in a new way
Waiting for them to break.

A game is what they play
Unaware of the
true
deep
dark
pain
this world brings.
The world they created.

The press of a button changes their fate:
Whether they're rich or poor,
Ecstatic, depressed
Healthy or infest with little loaded guns.

They've tricked us, but you don't know it.

You may think I'm lying.
Am I?

Never

Never shall I forget that day,
the day I left my grandmother on her deathbed,
after she asked me to stay.

Never shall I forget that plea.

Never shall I forget the fear in her eyes
and the hopelessness in her voice as
she transformed into such a vulnerable person.

Never shall I forget the emptiness that found me
that day and never left.

Never shall I forget the silence of the room as
I turned away and the pain that spread
with every pump of my heart.

Never shall I forget that moment that murdered
my hope since I knew that nothing,
not even her heartbroken family,
could make her fight to see another day.

Never shall I forget the darkness of that hospital
room,

mirroring my soul.

Never.

- After Elie Wiesel, "Never Shall I Forget"

I am a target.

There is a big red and white target on my back.
My back bears the burden of it, as person after person,
and event after event, hit the bullseye.

I am a target.
I don't know why.

Terrible people gravitate toward me.
And they tear me to shreds.

Maybe it's because I have self respect.
Or because I'm neither a man nor a proper lady.

I don't know why life is so cruel to me.
What did I do to deserve such a hard life,
when I'm only in high school?

For Granted

Why do we take life for granted?
This world is a terrifying place.
There is violence and hatred everywhere.
The simplest move can become your biggest nightmare.

So why do we...
Never remember to make that phone call?
Fail to set up that lunch date?
Have our kids worry more about college than having a childhood?
Waste time being someone we aren't?
Stay in unhappy and unhealthy relationships for convenience?
Not take that leap of faith toward falling in love with something or someone?
Forget that this world is also full of love if you look deep enough?

What are we waiting for?

A Dream Deffered

A dream deffered
Gets lost between Zoom calls,
Homework assignments
And Netflix binges.

A WWE star knocks it
down your priority list.

The feet of society squash it
until it can barely survive.

A more practical path sells itself
to you for the bargain price of
your happiness.

A side of regret comes with
every meal.

That choice was supposed to ease
your stress, instead it ruined
your life.

- After Langston Hughes, "Harlem"

My First Love

I fell in love at the age of 7.
This love traveled with me room to room
And consumed my every thought and free moment.
I was never happy when I was alone.

My first love was literature.
Reading and writing were my favorite things to do.
I zipped through books in mere days.
I wrote every single day about my childhood adventures.

That love has never left,
But it has changed.

I don't have all the time in the word to read and write.
I write for school and for my writing class,
But rarely for me.
I read textbooks and articles to maintain a proper lens of the world,
But never for fun.
I grow as a formulaic, argumentative writer,
But my writer's voice has yet to develop.

I write personal narratives,
But still fear being vulnerable on the page.

I'm fighting for the day to be that little girl again
For that is when I will be infatuated again.

Once Upon a Time

Once Upon a Time,

I was a little girl who wore pigtails
And acted like an adult.

I twirled down the street
And skipped down the halls.

I read at recess
And wrote stories in art class.

I watched my parent's wedding video instead of movies
And listened to the Beach Boys.

I screamed at the sky
And smiled with the ocean.

I miss that little girl.

She woke up at 6 AM for fun
And ate ice cream after school every day.

She fell asleep to Grey's Anatomy
And stole her dad's spot in bed.

She ran to the door when her favorite people
came home
And she asked if they had an A+ day.

I am her.
She is me.
But I miss her.

Lingering Completion

When I first met you,
My eyes lingered
And so did my heart
And so did my soul
Because I knew there
Was something between us
And I'm sorry it took me
So long to find it.

Now, I find myself
Laying in bed
Watching the latest Netflix hit
When melancholy washes over me
With a sad, longing feeling
For that hug,
That kiss,
That love.
How can I feel completely myself
When my heart is with someone else?

That brings loneliness.
Loneliness came with love.

Can't be lonely until
Someone teaches you
What it's like not to be.

The Spiral Staircase of My Mind

I've been running up and down these stairs for
16 years.
"I need to go grocery shopping"
Up 2 steps
"Oh my God, I forgot to do my math homework"
Down 3 stairs
"What am I going to have for breakfast?"
Up 10 steps
"Mom, I forgot to tell you...
Anyway, I have to do my math homework"
Down 12 stairs

My mind moves up, down, left and right
All
Day
L
O
N
G

The lists and calendars help,

but my comedic genius cannot be portrayed
via list or an anecdotal text message.
And it would take ages to write it all down for
later.

The spiral shot up in elementary school
when boredom allowed my imagination to run
wild.

My mind has since tamed the imagination,
but the spiral staircase did not stop with it.

Grief, stress, heartbreak, happiness, motivation
fuel the gears of the staircase.

If I can't tame my own thoughts,
how am I supposed to tame my own life?

Cerulean

the reflection of the daytime sky over the oceans
a section of my patchwork jeans
my outfit from head to toe on violence
awareness days
the train cars in my neighborhood
my beaten up SUV "Dempsey"
the representation of math class
a highlighter in my pencil case
my tongue after a cotton candy lollipop
a terrycloth towel swirled in my hair
the fast food cup housing my soda
my most used apps, Zoom and Google Docs
the hat of a newborn baby
the right, but actually left, side of a political map
my boyfriend's favorite shade
my middle school backpack
a recital rose

I Will

I will raise my voice for
the girls that have been through
too much, too young,
just like me.

I will scream for the right to an
abortion in all cases because no
young, unprepared, or traumatized person
should bear a child they cannot care for.

I will stand before every committee
until the female identifying students
in my school, including myself,
are treated equally.

I will plead so menstrual products
are free in every school and public place,
because menstruation is not a choice.

I will fight for myself and for others until there
is nothing left to fight for.

RBG & Me

When I heard of RBG's passing,
I sobbed from the pure heartbreak.

Her legacy was shadowed by the looming
anticipation of her replacement.

Amy Coney Barrett.

The Antithesis of Ruth Bader Ginsburg.

A disgrace to her legacy.
A threat to the rights of women.
Immigrants.
People of Color.
America.

But when people hear Barrett's name,
they do not think of her work.
They think of the work that came before her;
revolutionary, precedent-setting, remarkable.

So I hope that when I die,
my work will have touched someone
enough to create the same reaction.

At The Break of Day

In two years,
When all the AP work is done,
my high school clubs are under new leadership,
I'll never taste an abysmal school lunch again,
I've made it across the stage
And my tassel makes it to the other side,

The tears shed and
opportunities passed up
Will all be worth is because
My life will finally be
At the break of day.

Sunrise In Ethiopia

When I get to be a journalist,
A newspaper will be my canvas
Words, my paint,
And I will create masterpieces about
The Sunrise In Ethiopia
rising from mountain tops.

I'm gonna put some laughter in
And the blazing run's buzz,
An Amharic sentence's rasp.
The whoosh of a soccer ball catching air,
A blend of spices boiling over an open flame,
A village's kindness,
The scent of an icy breeze from far away.

I'm gonna put a little love in
And the weaving of my fingers and an infant's,
The sound of trees moving in the wind,
My new friend's bright smile,
The coarse dirt slipping into my shoes,
A working mother's song,
A vibrant bird's chirp,
The warmth of being part of a community.

I'm anticipating the day I

Change my soul,
Then talk about
The travels of my journalist self
And write about
Sunrise in Ethiopia.

- After Langston Hughes, "Daybreak in Alabama"